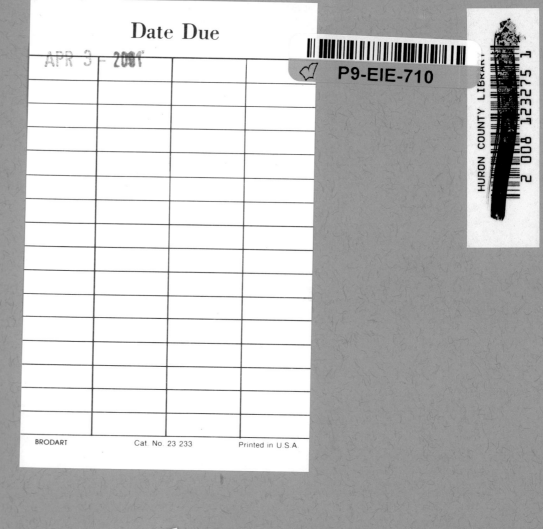

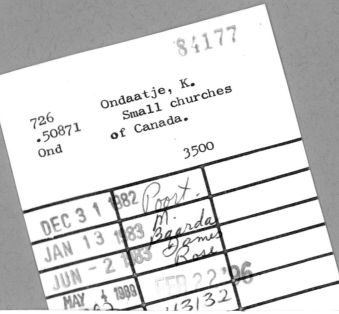

SMALL CHURCHES OF CANADA

SMALL CHURCHES OF CANADA

KIM ONDAATJE

LESTER & ORPEN DENNYS, PUBLISHERS

CANADIAN CATALOGUING IN PUBLICATION DATA
Ondaatje, Kim
    Small churches of Canada

Bibliography: p.
ISBN 0-88619-016-9

1. Churches – Canada – Pictorial works.   I. Title.

NA5240.052   726'.50971   C82-094530-7

Printed Norgraphics (Canada) Limited.
Bound Hunter Rose Company Ltd.
Typesetting Alpha Graphics Limited
Colour separations Colourgraph Reproduction Inc.
Production Paula Chabanais Productions
Design C. Wilson/Sunkisst Graphics

Printed and bound in Canada for
Lester & Orpen Dennys Limited
78 Sullivan Street
Toronto, Ontario M5T 1C1

BIBLIOGRAPHY

Angus, Margaret. *The Old Stones of Kingston.* Toronto: University of Toronto Press, 1966.

Berton, Laura Beatrice. *I Married the Klondike.* Toronto: McClelland and Stewart, 1977.

Hohn, Hubert (ed). *Byzantine Churches of Alberta.* (Photographs by Orest Semchishen.) Edmonton: Edmonton Art Gallery, 1976.

Hett, Francis Paget. *Georgina: A Type Study of Early Settlement and Church Building in Upper Canada.* Sutton West: Paget Press, 1978.

Kalman, Harold D. *Pioneer Churches.* (Photographs by John de Visser.) Toronto: McClelland and Stewart, 1976.

MacRae, Marion, and Anthony Adamson. *Hallowed walls: church architecture of Upper Canada.* Toronto: Clarke, Irwin and Company Limited, 1975.

Veillette, John, and Gary White. *Early Indian Village Churches.* Vancouver: University of British Columbia Press, 1977.

Woodall, Ronald, and T.H. Watkins. *Taken by the Wind: Vanishing Architecture of the West.* Don Mills: General Publishing Co. Limited, 1977.

JACKET PHOTOS:
Front Memorial Chapel, Roman Catholic Cemetery
    St. Jérôme, P.Q.
Back Derelict Anglican Church
    Rockingham, Ont.

This book is dedicated
to my Family and my Friends
and all those strangers who
helped me along the way —
without all these people
nothing I do would be possible.

Foreword

his book began in Prince Edward Island on a grey day in early spring. An exhibition of my paintings and prints had just opened at Confederation Centre in Charlottetown, and Moncrieff Williamson, the director, and his wife Pamela, were driving me around the island. Wherever we went that day, my eye was caught by little white churches set like solitaires in the gently rolling hills or nestled between the fields of freshly ploughed red earth.

When I returned to Ontario, where I was taking photographs of old houses for a film and a book, I began to notice the little churches there as well. Several outstanding ones crept into the book, *Old Ontario Houses*, and by the time that project was completed my next one had already begun. I was travelling farther and farther afield to seek out small churches and chapels. I was in love with them.

Unlike cathedrals and large churches, which tend to be sophisticated and eclectic — because they have been designed by church architects, and built and added to over a long period of time — little churches were usually built in a matter of months, out of simple materials, by a few men. Because the builders brought from their homelands definite ideas about how a place of worship should look and what it should contain, these churches and chapels reflect a great diversity of religious and ethnic background. They show how varied our roots are — how varied, and how interwoven. The onion domes of Greek and Russian Orthodox tradition are found not just on the Prairies but also along the expressways of Ontario. The fleur-de-lis emblem turns up frequently in the mission churches of British Columbia, and in Vancouver there is a Chinese Mennonite meeting house. I was surprised to find that pioneers from Iceland had built a Lutheran church on the Manitoba prairie, and in a Saskatchewan town I ran across a church for the followers of the Swedish mystic Emanuel Swedenborg.

Many of the little churches I stumbled upon were locked or boarded up, and bore no identifying sign. Some of these, in resort areas, are used only during the summer months. Others stand, alone and derelict, as solitary symbols of villages long since disappeared; no doubt neighbouring farmers and vandals have pillaged the other buildings of the town, but — out of respect, or perhaps superstition — the church has been left untouched. Sometimes I was lucky enough to find people who knew the church's history, and could tell me stories of the pioneers and missionaries and Indians who had played a part in it. But often there was no one around. Several times I met people living next door to an outstanding chapel who had no idea of its name, its denomination, or when it had been built; other times I collected a lot of information from various local sources, only to find much of it conflicting.

Sometimes, after driving miles to reach a special church, I found that the church had vanished: I arrived at the site of a Doukhobor prayer house in British Columbia two weeks after it had been burned to the ground by feuding members. Other churches proved impossible to photograph for one reason or another. For example, the famous Stollen church at Windermere, British Columbia, is not included because it was undergoing renovations when I reached it and was sheathed in scaffolding.

One could spend a lifetime criss-crossing this country and still not come across all the outstanding little churches. I spent five years, and although I travelled many thousands of miles, in every kind of weather and by every means of transport, there were some — like the derelict stone chapel at Pelly Bay, up on the Gulf of Boothia near Baffin Island — that I couldn't get to; I just couldn't devote that much time and money to a single church.

Even so, I found by the end of my travels that I had collected hundreds of photographs, far more than I could include in this book. I hate playing God in the vegetable patch, thinning out the carrots — this one lives, that one dies — but many of the pictures had to go. (Some will appear in a film I am making, and I shall be using others in my lectures.)

Most of the pictures that appear here were chosen for their visual interest, but a few are included because of some intriguing legend or anecdote associated with them. The text is drawn from the information I was given locally — as far as I felt it was reliable — and from what books I could find on the subject. In the bibliography I list the few that were helpful.

I am an artist — not an architect or a historian. I have put together this collection because of the charm and fascination that these small churches and chapels hold for me. I hope that you who read the book will find the same pleasure in them, and that some of you may perhaps be lured into going out and finding more of these little churches, as yet undiscovered.

I have a knack for getting into difficult situations. When I was stranded in the Yukon by ice fog, sky-hiking in the Arctic, stuck in the spring mud in Newfoundland, driven off the road by a logging truck in British Columbia, caught in a white-out on the Bruce Peninsula — when I found my car without brakes in Manitoba or with a broken fan-belt far up the Saguenay — I was only able to cope because of the help of strangers. They provided the necessary assistance; they gave me food, shelter, and information; they also relieved the loneliness of my work. I am grateful to them all.

I would like to thank the juries of the Canada Council Explorations Program and the Ontario Arts Council, whose research grants made much of my travel possible, and the Outreach Program in British Columbia.

I am most indebted to Henry Yee, who does all my photographic prints; to Lola Tostevin, who travelled with me through Quebec acting as translator; to Steven Behal and James Moyer, who did their best to teach me — a difficult student — the rules of photography; and to Christopher Whalley, who worked out my travel routes in the West. Many clergymen and archivists gave me information, as did friends like Nancy Lee Patterson and Lois Mackenzie. I am most grateful to Lynn Bourdages, who for years has assisted my family and household during my necessary absences. I want to thank Marjorie Shumilo, who typed the manuscript on short notice when I turned up at a quiet inn in Niagara-on-the-Lake to work my way through the home stretch. And finally I want to thank the designer, Catherine Wilson, and all at Lester & Orpen Dennys.

PHOTO: STEVE BEHAL

The author at the Church of St. Michael and All Angels, Spences Bridge, B.C.

Introduction

oots, and the desire for them, are spoken of with longing mainly by the dispossessed. It's the cosmopolitan who falls in love with the countryside—like A.J. Casson, born in Toronto, who painted an enduring record of rural Ontario in towns like Elora, Alton, and Cheltenham, and crystallized "a mood that would otherwise be lost". Small towns had been part of Casson's childhood—as a boy he often visited Meadowvale (today almost swallowed up by Toronto)—and in returning to seek out those roots he fell in love with the small-town feeling. Much the same hunger for experience remembered sent Kim Ondaatje on the journey of discovery that is the subject of this book.

Ondaatje was born and raised in the city, but spent long summers in northern Ontario. Her father, the late Frank M. Kimbark, ran a successful printing business. A draughtsman himself, he collected etchings and engravings and hung them, sometimes four rows high, in the family's big stone house in North Toronto. Her mother, Betty Browning Harris, was a ballet dancer who had worked with Pavlova's company, and she wanted her daughter to be a dancer or an actress. But Kim's interest in the visual arts was stirred by her father's collection, and by friendships with Canadian artists like Yvonne McKague Housser, Marian Scott, and Isabel McLaughlin. She made up her mind that she would be a painter.

After graduating from Toronto's Havergal College she enrolled at the Ontario College of Art, but when she had finished the basic training course, Harley Parker—then head of drawing and painting—advised her to go to university, where she could study literature, philosophy, psychology, and history. She was a natural-born painter, he said; she'd paint later. She enrolled at McGill and completed a BA program in English, marrying poet D.G. Jones while she was still an undergraduate. She went on to Queen's on a teaching fellowship for her MA and then taught English at Waterloo and Sherbrooke universities, as well as having four children along the way. She and Jones eventually divorced.

In 1963 she married poet Michael Ondaatje. She gave up her teaching career and had two more children, and it was at this time that she began to paint again. Her early pictures revealed the influence of various painters she admired, like David B. Milne and Paul-Emile Borduas. The style was impressionistic and abstract, and the techniques ranged from heavy impasto to slashes of paint applied with the knife. Her mature work did not begin to appear until 1967, when she was in London, Ontario, and being encouraged in her art by realist painter Jack Chambers.

The Ondaatje family was living in an old house on Piccadilly Street, and she began to use its interior in her paintings and prints. It was then that she really began to "see", mostly in bits that tantalized, images that provided clues, hints, and suggestions: rooms seen through empty rooms, paintings within paintings, mirrors in mirrors. The fifteen acrylic paintings and nine prints in the suite *The House on Piccadilly Street* are not nostalgic, in any sentimental sense, but reveal her profound fascination with the details and feeling of an old Ontario house. "I try to get the viewer to wonder who lives in the places I paint, what the people are like, what happened before the painting, what will happen after," she says. The effect is invariably tranquil, like water running silently over rocks. Often— and this applies to her photographs as well as her paintings—the images are distanced, and have a sense of vacancy.

The unusual course Ondaatje followed to become an artist informs all her work—painting, prints, films, and photographs. She always has a lyric quality. She often quotes Emily Dickinson's lines, "There's a certain slant of light... when it comes, the landscape listens." It's no surprise that Dickinson is one of her favourite poets: Ondaatje's work is similarly clear-cut, sparse, and focused, but with the same underlying passion.

Ondaatje is no miniaturist; she strives for the monumental. In this collection of photographs many of the churches are central images, while trees, roads, and fences serve as frames, exaggerating the size of the subjects and placing them in the context of the landscape. As in the *Factory* series, twelve paintings and seven prints of industrial plants which she developed from 1970 to 1974, she concentrates on geometric forms. But the effect is never cold or impersonal. On the contrary, she invites the viewer to walk into her work; indeed she often includes a way of entering, like a road. It's a kind of participatory democracy in art: she wants to share her unique way of seeing.

Ondaatje points out to us many fascinating and visually exciting features of the churches she has discovered across the country. But her vision is deeper than this—behind the structural oddities and the curious decorative motifs, the ingenious adaptations and the architectural crossbreeding, she sees the people who have come together here, from all around the world, bringing to this vast and empty land the richness of their traditions, the courage of their resolve, and—above all—the strength of their abiding faith.

Joan Murray
Director, Robert McLaughlin Gallery
Oshawa, Ontario

SMALL CHURCHES OF CANADA

ROMAN CATHOLIC MEMORIAL CHAPEL
ST. JOHN'S, NFLD.

This little chapel, boarded up for winter, stands in the middle of the Catholic cemetery on Kennas Hill.

The small size and wooden construction of this white building set against an Eastern Townships forest is a clue to its Protestant affiliation. The Roman Catholic congregations have torn down almost all their small log or wooden churches, and have replaced them with edifices of brick or stone that dominate the landscape. I did find modest Catholic memorial chapels, and a few abandoned processional chapels on Ile d'Orléans and along the north shore of the St. Lawrence, but except for those nearly all the small churches I found in Quebec were Protestant. Several had signs indicating that the building was shared by members of the Anglican and United churches.

Clearly visible from the "old Banff highway", this chapel was named after the Reverend Frank McDougall, the first Protestant missionary to reach the territory now known as Alberta. McDougall, a Methodist, arrived in southern Alberta in 1840. In 1873 his son John began work on the church, which was completed a year or two later. It is a simple building without any distinctive features other than the pointed peaks on the windows and over the door. The tower was added at a later date. In January of 1867 the Reverend McDougall lost his way on the prairie, and his frozen body was not found until February. He is buried beside this church. The fence which appears to be herding people inside actually serves to keep out grazing cattle.

St. Nicholas Anglican
Kennell, Sask.

St. Nicholas is a little chapel nestled among the hills on the east side of the Qu'Appelle Valley a few miles north of Regina. It now stands all by itself; the town of Kennell which once surrounded it has vanished. St. Nicholas was built by a local carpenter around 1895, and has been beautifully maintained or restored.

Facing S<small>T</small>. S<small>AVIOUR'S</small> A<small>NGLICAN</small>
B<small>ARKERVILLE</small>, B.C.

Barkerville was named after Billy Barker, a prospector who, in August of 1862, made the richest strike in British Columbia's history. The town sprang up around Billy's claim. It was destroyed by fire in 1868 but rebuilt in 1869, and careful maintenance and renovation have preserved its charm. St. Saviour's Anglican Church, which was built during the 1869 reconstruction, has slender Gothic windows and vertical board-and-batten siding which blend perfectly with the spruce spires on the hill behind. St. Saviour's, which I understand is the oldest Anglican church in British Columbia, is no longer in regular use, but it is a favourite place for weddings and other special services during the warmer months. As for Billy Barker, he squandered his fortune and died penniless in an old folks' home.

A*bove* S<small>T</small>. S<small>TEPHEN'S</small> A<small>NGLICAN</small>
T<small>ELKWA</small>, B.C.

The Reverend Stephenson, described to me as "the best sky-pilot ever to wear a pair of boots", was stationed in Atlin, in the far north-west corner of British Columbia, when his bishop ordered him to build a church down in the Bulkley Valley. A powerful six-footer, Stephenson shouldered a sixty-pound back pack — filled mainly with books, according to the tale — and hiked over five hundred miles down the Yukon Telegraph Trail to Telkwa, a lumber town on the shores of the Bulkley River (now on Highway 16 between Smithers and Houston). He arrived there in 1910 and managed to persuade the mill owners, Roman Catholic and Protestant alike, to donate lumber for the church. He began building at once, with the help of the local residents, and the church was finished in 1911; the bell and lych-gate were added in 1921.

TRYON UNITED
TRYON, P.E.I.

The best-known church architect in Prince Edward Island was William Critchlow Harris, the brother of artist Robert Harris who painted the famous portrait of the Fathers of Confederation. Many William Harris churches can be found around the island, but Tryon United is one of his simplest, and it is my personal favourite. The tall steeple with its gables housing Gothic vents around the drum (the part that houses the bell) is one of the features of a Harris church; another is the use of buttresses — usually fake ones like these — which are decorative exterior supports of the church and tower walls. Harris himself described this church, which was originally Methodist, as "decent and a little severe, calculated to satisfy rather than excite".

ROMAN CATHOLIC SHRINE
LEBRET, SASK.

This shrine on the hillside above the town of Lebret, Saskatchewan, was built in 1919 to commemorate those who died in World War I. The first mass was held in it in 1921. In 1928 the shrine and all the statues were burned. (When I asked about the shrine and its history at the post office, I was told that some members of the Ku Klux Klan were suspected to have been responsible for the burning.) The present shrine with the Way of the Cross leading up to it was built in 1929.

DOUKHOBOR PRAYER HOUSE
VEREGIN, SASK.

The Doukhobors first arrived in Canada in 1899, after being driven out of Russia for their rejection of military service and civil authority. As they believe in simplicity and equality, most of their meeting houses are plain, rather uninteresting buildings. The one in Veregin, built in 1917, is an exception: it looks more like a Louisiana plantation house. What appears from a distance to be delicate gingerbread is really fine metal-work cut by J. J. Mahonin. The main floor of the building was used for meetings and prayer services, and Peter Veregin, the leader of the community, lived on the second floor; the church is now the museum of the Doukhobor Society of Veregin.

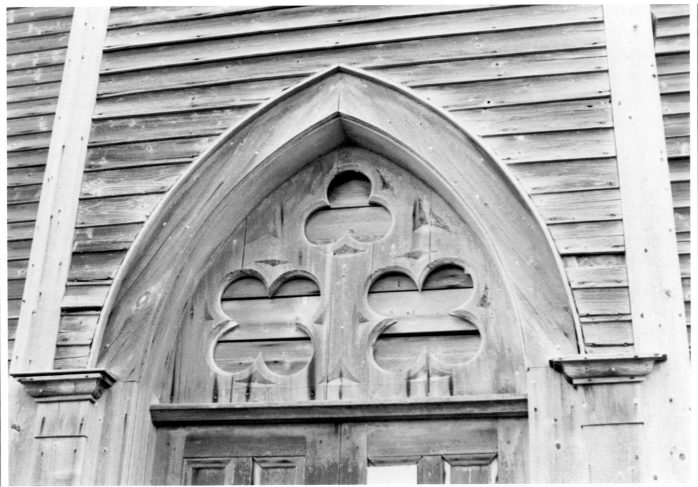

T his silvered wood beauty lies just
off the Cabot Trail a couple of miles
south of Chéticamp, Nova Scotia. The
churchyard is overgrown with wild
cherry trees and bushes.

Frelsis Lutheran Church was built in 1889, only eight years after the first five families of Icelandic pioneers struggled through a fierce March blizzard to their uncleared homesteads north of what is now Baldur, Manitoba. It was placed on the brow of a hill in southern Manitoba, and furnished with a hand-carved pulpit, chandeliers, an organ, and a 500-pound copper bell that could be heard for five miles. Its name, "Frelsis", means "Liberty". The weatherworn little church is now protected as a historical building — it is the oldest standing Icelandic church in Canada — and it remains a monument to the determination and craftsmanship of the settlers who built it.

ST. JOHN'S UNITED
MOUNT STEWART, P.E.I.

In all my travels across this country, I could not help finding favourites among the many churches I photographed. This is one of them. The use of the five-pointed star, in the bull's-eye window over the door and in the Gothic peaks of the windows and entrance, is the first thing to catch your eye. As you approach the double doors of the entrance you notice the panelling and, in spite of the subtle white paint, the arrows in the upper panels pointing heavenwards. Inside the church is light and airy, decorated with yellow stars set strikingly in royal blue circles within the crimson peaks of the windows. The wooden interior walls, with vertical wainscotting below and slender horizontal boards above, are soft white, the window and door frames are yellow ochre, and the ceiling is varnished brown. The pews of blond vertical boards are outlined with darker wood along the top and on the armrests, and a dark gold rug runs down the aisles. As in many churches on the island, there is a balcony at the back, but in place of the usual railing are low white horizontal panels.

Ontario has a number of interesting little chapels in the midst of cemeteries. They range from the Glenwood Memorial Chapel in Picton, with its decorative tin shingling, to the famous little blue church near Prescott at Maitland. My own favourite is this

little one at Port Hope, built in 1891 by James "Yankee" Guest as a memorial for his wife Patience who had died in 1880. It's painted the colour of rich cream, with dark green trim, and has a simple neatness which is neither austere nor boring. The hood over the door, the peaks of the windows, and the peak of the gable and the tiny bell tower (not shown) all match perfectly, while the double door with its vertical lines somehow complements the horizontal pattern of the siding.

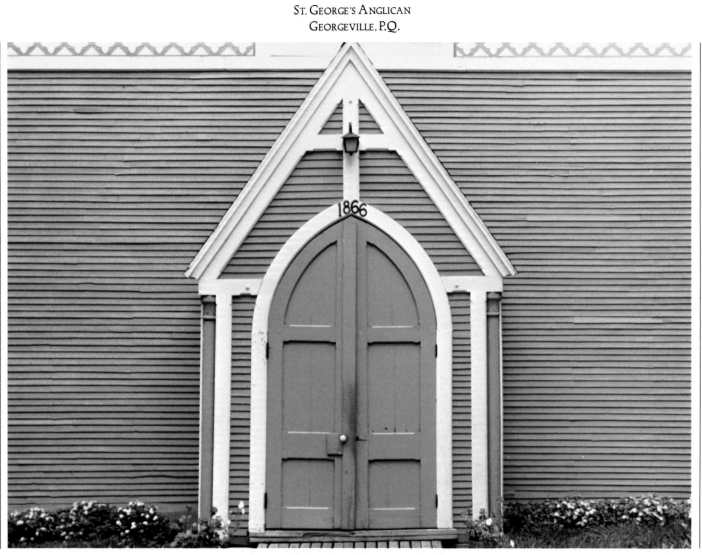

One of the most attractive churches in the Eastern Townships is this one, with its narrow horizontal siding painted a serene grey and white. The date of the church's completion is clearly visible over the original doors of the main entrance.

All Saints fascinates me, and I couldn't resist including it even though it is a little large for a "small" church. It has one of the most elaborate wooden ceilings I've seen, and the exterior of the church — like the ceiling — is painted in such a way that all the decorative and architectural features stand out dramatically.

ALL SAINTS' ANGLICAN
ST. ANDREW'S-BY-THE-SEA, N.B.

T he bell tower of All Saints' Anglican is most impressive, for it has unusually tall false buttresses which remind me of extension aerials because each section gets progressively slimmer as it goes up. Tucked between two central buttresses on either side is a small bull's-eye window which looks like a doily. The church was built in 1867, of native spruce and pine, and cost twelve thousand dollars — a price which did not include the furnishings or the stained-glass windows.

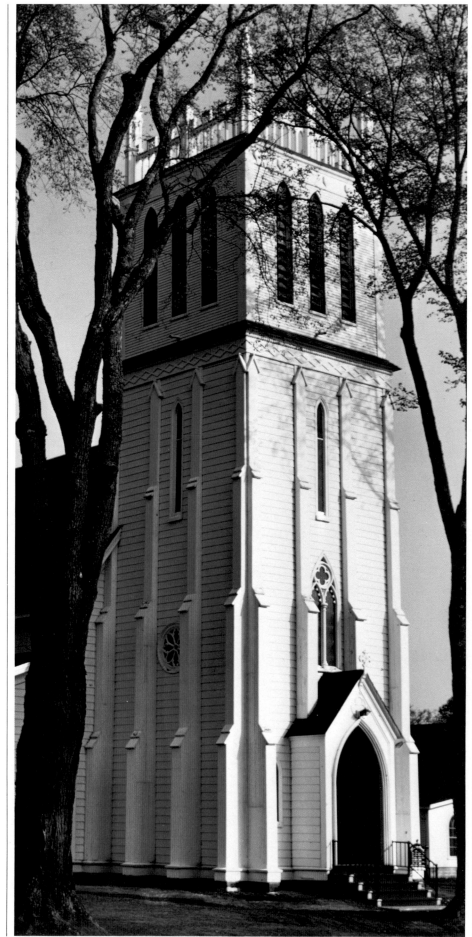

This striking chapel was recon-structed and expanded in the mid-seventies by John Veillette and Gary White, authors of *Early Indian Village Churches*, with a crew of local carpenters and summer-student employees. I reached Glen Vowell in a snowstorm and was unable to find anyone around to let me into the church. Since I had read about the reconstruction of the interior as well as the exterior in Veil-lette and White's book it was disap-pointing, but seeing the exterior of the church was well worth the trip.

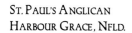

S tone churches are rare in Newfoundland and this one at Harbour
Grace, with its iron gates and delicate
arch, is quite exceptional. Much of the
stonework has been restored. I
remember noticing some lovely little
doors inside that led to the balcony.

The body of Greenock Church is quite plain — the interior resembles that of St. Andrew's at Niagara-on-the-Lake with its box stalls, U-shaped balcony, and spacious open feeling — but Greenock's Christopher Wren –style steeple is one of the most unusual in the country. Its embellishments include a weathervane, a star-faced clock, classical trim under the eaves, and a curious relief painting of a tree in full leaf. Many people mistake this for the Tree of Life or the Tree of Knowledge, but in fact it is an oak tree, and was placed on the tower as a symbol of Greenock, the Scottish birthplace of Captain Christopher Scott. According to local tradition, in 1822 the Presbyterians were taunted by the Anglicans for not having a church of their own; Captain Scott was so incensed by their remarks that he personally financed the building of the church and, upon its completion in 1824, named it after his hometown.

St. Ann's was built around 1910 to serve the Chuchuwayha Indian Reserve. It stands on a hill overlooking the Similkameen River, south-west of Penticton, in central British Columbia. Its most attractive features are the slender arched windows and the repetitions of these arches in the bell tower. At the time the church was built the population on the Reserve was barely thirty. When a Reserve is as small as this, a priest only gets around three or four times a year, for he has to cover a circuit of hundreds of miles and serve thousands of people.

Holy Ascension Church, now derelict, was built by poor immigrants in 1905. Like the church built some five years later in Sirko, Manitoba (see page 78), Holy Ascension resembles an Eastern European peasant cottage. It has a sloping roof with low overhanging eaves — although the roof is shingled, rather than thatched as a cottage roof would be — and a plain dirt floor. The log construction is also simple, with the logs saddle-notched rather than dovetailed or form-fitted. Only the window with its lovely touch of primitive Gothic, the three-sided sanctuary at the end, and the plain crosses indicate that this is in fact a church.

Facing UKRAINIAN GREEK ORTHODOX
NEAR WAKAW, SASK.

About six miles south of Wakaw is this church, which struck me as exceptional for several reasons. For one thing, the bell tower is attached to the church, whereas just about all the other bell towers I saw in the west were free-standing. I was also intrigued by the number of small domes clustered around the large central one, and by the cemetery which made me think of a chess board. Considering the quantity of windows in the central dome I am sure the church must have been flooded with light, but unfortunately the doors were locked and there was no one around to tell me where I might find the key.

Many western churches are tucked into the corners of fields; this is because the land has been donated by a local farmer.

St. Vladimir Ukrainian Greek Orthodox
Vegreville, Alta.

Of all the many Greek and Russian Orthodox churches I visited in the west, this is the one I like best. It is more or less typical in design: it has the large onion dome with windows to let in light just at the point where the two wings intersect to form a cross, the small domed twin towers on either side of the entrance, and the free-standing bell tower beside the church. Inside, however, the church is exceptional, for it has unusually fine paintings and decorative motifs by Waldym W. Dobrolige. These include a panel depicting a massive baptism, and double-winged angels in the archways over the columns. The scroll-work in the borders and panels is also delicate and reminds me of the illuminations on old manuscripts. I hear that there is a plan to move the church to a museum village; I hope it can be done without any damage to the building or its art.

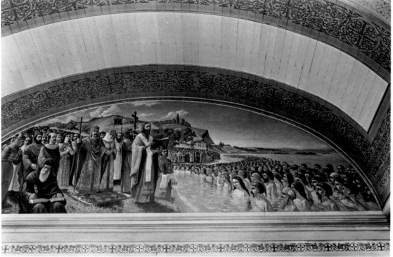

ST. JOHN'S ANGLICAN
LUNENBERG, N.S.

The original St. John's is said to have been the second Anglican church built in North America; the first was built in Jamestown, Virginia, prior to 1610. Both were of log construction, and neither has survived. The current St. John's has the appearance of a very large church, but it began as a small one; extensions have been added along either side of the main building within the past century.

Our Lady of Rosemary,
Roman Catholic
Burwash Landing, Yukon

This log church was built in 1943 by Father Morisset of the Oblate Order of Mary the Immaculate — an order that has done a great deal of work in the north and north-west. The rectory, on the left side of the picture, was added in 1950. Services take place only during the summer months. I talked with an elderly woman, Jessie Joe, who lives in the Indian village and has been a member of the church from the start. Her eyes smiled as she remembered Father Morisset. She described the excitement of the village children whenever his truck appeared, and explained that he not only taught them lessons but took them berry-picking and squirrel-hunting. When parents were out on the trap-lines for months at a time he would come and check with whoever was looking after the children to see that they had enough to eat; if not, he'd go and get a special permit and shoot a moose for them. In the north the past and present merge: many of the men who created history — or legends — are still living, and when I last heard, Father Morisset was continuing his work in Whitehorse.

ST. PETER'S-ON-THE-ROCK, ANGLICAN
STONY LAKE, ONT.

The first Anglican services at Stony Lake, near Lakefield, were held on the veranda of Archdeacon Mackenzie's cottage, but the congregation made up their minds to build a real summer church. The result, finished in 1913, was St. Peter's and, adjoining it, "Clergy Cottage", for the attending clergyman and his family. The unique character of this tiny summer church was aptly described by one member of the congregation: "It isn't everywhere that you can fish out the window if you don't like the sermon."

ST. ANNE'S ROMAN CATHOLIC
COWICHAN, B.C.

The original St. Anne's, a log chapel, was built in 1859 by Father Pierre Rondeault. It was replaced by him in 1869 with this stone structure which became known as the "butter church" because Father Rondeault paid for the stonework and carpentry out of proceeds from his butter farm. When the congregation moved to a new and larger church in 1880, the doors and windows were removed and placed in other Roman Catholic churches. For a number of years the building was cared for, but it was abandoned during the war years and has stood, derelict but still beautiful, ever since. Some restoration was done during the seventies; when I was there the masonry had been restored and a historical plaque was on the building.

OUR LADY OF THE WAY ROMAN CATHOLIC
HAINES JUNCTION, YUKON

During the Second World War, when American troops were building the Alaska Highway across the Yukon Territory, they put up temporary camps along the route. In the fifties a discarded Quonset hut from that period was turned into this chapel. Unusual as it may be, Our Lady of the Way has the same characteristics as many other Yukon churches: it is small and therefore reasonably easy to heat, and it was built quickly out of the materials available.

Father Morisset, who built the log church at Burwash Landing (see p. 36), is responsible for this little chapel as well. In having the Quonset hut hauled out of the bush where it had been dumped and turning it into this ingenious church, he revealed the resourcefulness typical of the clergy who serve in the north. It was a beautifully clear morning in February when I first saw Our Lady of the Way. The sun was catching the tiny star on top of the cross, and it gleamed a dazzling white against the shadow blues of the St. Elias mountains, the tallest in Canada.

Above CHRIST CHURCH ANGLICAN
UPPER CANADA VILLAGE, MORRISBURG, ONT.

Facing HOLLOWAY MEMORIAL CHAPEL
POINT ABINO, NEAR PORT COLBORNE, ONT.

Christ Church was moved to Upper Canada Village from Moulinette, a village which vanished in the course of the St. Lawrence Seaway project. Adam Dixon, a wealthy mill owner, donated the land on which this handsome little church was originally built and also paid for its construction. Ironically, according to local legend the first service held in Christ Church was for Dixon's funeral in May, 1837.

In accordance with the wishes of the original donors, this little chapel is not only interdenominational but international as well: services are conducted, by invitation, by both Canadian and American clergymen of various faiths. The country-style chapel was built in 1894 by Mary Ann Holloway in memory of her parents, on land owned by her brother Allan. In 1930 the chapel was moved to its present

site near the yacht club on the margin of Lake Erie. It was deeded to the church by Allan Holloway and remodelled along the more formal lines of a New England village church. In 1951 a local resident purchased more land for the chapel and donated funds for additions including a bride's room , a minister's room, and washrooms. The chapel is still in use during the summer months and is a favourite setting for weddings and christenings.

St. Anthony's Roman Catholic
Fort Steele, B.C.

Father Coccola was greatly respected by the Indians of the Kootenay area for his courage, and they had helped him to build the majestic St. Eugene Mission Church. In June of 1897, when his bishop asked him to build a small church in nearby Fort Steele, he again called on his Indian friends. St. Anthony's opened its doors on October 31, 1897, just a little over four months after the bishop had issued his request. Most little churches are still heated by wood stoves; some of the stoves are more ornate than the one in St. Anthony's, while others are made out of old oil barrels. Nearly all the churches originally had oil or gas lamps, and although many of these have been converted to electricity the one at Fort Steele still burns kerosene.

Fort Selkirk, on the Yukon River between Dawson and Whitehorse, was a thriving community from the gold-rush era of the nineties until the days when caterpillar-track vehicles made their way north by creeping along the course of the frozen river, in the days before snowmobiles. Its public buildings consisted of two stores, a school, an Anglican church, an RCMP post, and a small Roman Catholic chapel; for a while, too, a regiment was stationed there. When the road from Whitehorse to Dawson was built it did not go anywhere near Fort Selkirk, and as the traffic flow moved from the river to the road the town's settlers found themselves more and more isolated. Gradually they moved elsewhere. Now the restored settlement — a favourite spot for summer visitors — has only two

residents, an Indian couple who are its caretakers. These photographs were taken in the winter of 1979, an exceptionally cold and snowy one in the Yukon; for the first time, the couple at the Fort told me, the dog team that makes an annual run from Dawson to the Rendez-vous winter festival in Whitehorse was unable to come. The snow was too deep for long-distance travel by snowmobile and I had to go in by helicopter. The little church is built out of small logs, since no large trees grow that far north, and when I saw it from the air, with its surrounding fields of snow and its one sentinel spruce, it looked like a Christmas card. The long shadows suggest to a southerner that the picture was taken in late afternoon, but actually it was shot at high noon; during the winter months the arctic sun rises and sets in the south and the shadows are always long.

When I came across this small chapel set back from the highway, there was absolutely no one I could ask about it; everyone was off watching or fighting a bush fire a few miles away. I can only say that it stands on the west side of the road outside Pelly's Crossing and is the only Anglican church in Canada with this name.

The day I photographed St. Paul's, with the overhanging spruce boughs swooping and swaying over the churchyard and the fence pickets standing up like white feathers amid the dark green, I felt a strange sort of presence. I've had a similar feeling before, around a number of the old mission chapels in British Columbia. It's as if the old spirits are still watching — overshadowed by Christianity, perhaps, but by no means banished.

Above ST. PAUL'S ANGLICAN, "HER MAJESTY'S CHAPEL OF THE MOHAWKS"
BRANTFORD, ONT.

Joseph Brant was chief of an Indian tribe in the New York region at the time of the American Revolution. He and his people fought loyally on the British side, and after the war they fled to south-western Ontario where they were eventually given a large tract of land along the Grand River. In 1785 the British government built them a wooden Anglican church on what is now the outskirts of Brantford (named for Chief Brant), and later George III donated a set of Royal Arms to the chapel. The building has been altered and restored over the years, but still stands on its original foundation and contains the original beams. It is the oldest church in Ontario in continuous use, and the only Indian chapel royally dedicated.

STE.-MARIE-AUX-HURONS, ROMAN CATHOLIC
MISSION CHAPEL
NEAR MIDLAND, ONT.

Hard upon the heels of explorers like Champlain came the courageous and uncompromising Jesuit missionaries, resolved to save the souls of the "heathen" Indians at any price. Around 1630 Fathers Jean de Brébeuf and Gabriel Lalemant, among others, entered Huron territory around the south shores of Georgian Bay in order to found missions and build chapels for the converted. They succeeded in building one such chapel at Fort Ste. Marie — near the present town of Midland — in 1639. But Father Brébeuf had had premonitions of forthcoming doom: he had dreamed of a great cross slowly approaching from Iroquois territory, a cross he described to the other brothers as "large enough to crucify us all". In entering Huron territory the Jesuits had aroused the fury of the belligerent Iroquois, whom Father Lalemant had described in a letter as coming like foxes, attacking the lions, and taking flight "like birds, disappearing before they have really appeared." In 1649 the Iroquois attacked. Father Brébeuf and his fellow priests were captured and tortured to death. Father Brébeuf was buried beside his chapel at Fort Ste. Marie, but the chapel was burned to the ground shortly after. Brébeuf was canonized in 1930.

The Jesuits, with their love of graciousness, had valuable ornaments in even their remotest chapels, and the one at Fort Ste. Marie was no exception. Reports of visitors and writings in the Order's journal *Jesuit Relations* describe a painting, a statue, an elaborate cross, and an altar adorned with seven angels, and amid the rubble were found bits of coloured glass — evidence that stained-glass windows once defied the wilderness. This modern chapel is a simplified version of the original, and it lies within the grounds of the reconstructed fort.

CHURCH OF ST. MARY MAGDALEN, ROMAN
CATHOLIC
HAGWILGET, B.C.

This little church which sits up on top of a hill overlooking the Bulkley River Valley has a most unusual bull's-eye window decoration: a row of alternating forks and knives, cut out of wood and painted bright gold, follows the rim of the window creating a sunburst pattern. Decorations like this and (see next page) the cross over the church door at Tachie, north-west of Fort St. James, British

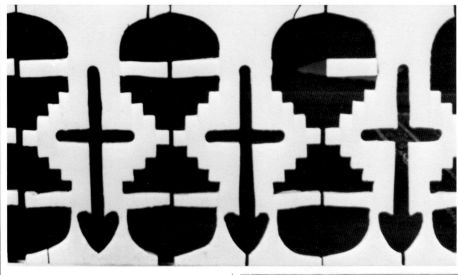

Columbia, as well as the ornamentation on the communion railings and steeples of Indian mission churches across Canada, reveal an interesting blend of Indian and Christian motifs and symbols.

Many of the mission churches, like the one at Pays Plat in northern Ontario with its unusual circular decoration in its steeple and its saint protected by plastic in its niche, were undergoing restoration; others remain derelict. Only a few are in regular use.

This tiny log chapel is located on the reserve at Pinchie, north-west of Fort St. James, which in turn is north-west of Prince George. Note the simple bell rack outside the church.

Facing LITTLE SANDS UNITED
LITTLE SANDS, P.E.I.

The bull's-eye window in the gable surprised me, as I took it for the Star of David, but someone explained that in this case the double triangle represented the Double Trinity. The porch here seemed most appropriate for a frame church by the sea.

St. Andrew's is an eye-catching building on the banks of the Red River. Its stone wall and gate were probably added after the First World War as the gate is really a memorial arch — the keystone contains a bust carved in relief of an "unknown soldier". The church itself was built in 1849, thirty-seven years after the first hardy settlers arrived from Scotland and Ireland under the direction of Thomas Douglas, the fifth Earl of Selkirk. They landed on the shores of Hudson Bay and had to survive the winter there before they could make their way up along the Nelson River, Lake Winnipeg, and the Red River to the large tract of land held by the Earl in the Winnipeg basin.

St. Andrew's is rich in stories. I was told that a sexton was murdered here, that dogs always bark as they approach, and — strangest of all — that ghosts, trying to find a way into the building, leave the grass around it trodden and flattened. Not far from the church is a rather large school which I imagine supplies St. Andrew's with plenty of ghosts.

Facing CONGREGATIONAL MEETING HOUSE,
NOW SHEFFIELD UNITED
SHEFFIELD, N.B.

In 1763 a group of Congregationalist settlers from Massachusetts established a community known as Maugerville along the banks of New Brunswick's St. John River. For a number of years they held their religious meetings in their homes, until in 1775 they built this meeting house with its unusual tower and steeple. (Many of the settlers were from Rawley, Massachusetts, and this meeting house is said to be a replica of the one in Rawley.) The following year brought the American Revolution, and the Maugerville Congregationalists found themselves surrounded by hostile Loyalists. They decided to move to Sheffield, five miles farther down the river, and to take their church with them. It took a hundred oxen to accomplish the feat, but — miraculously — the meeting house arrived at its new destination almost unharmed; only minor repairs to the steeple were needed.

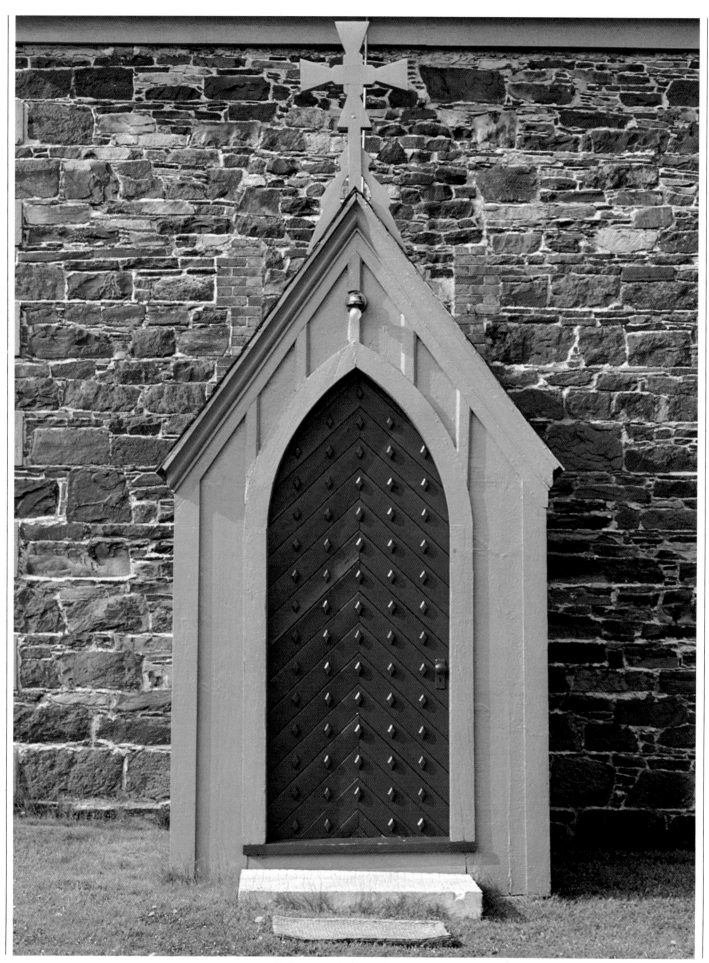

ST. JOHN THE BAPTIST, ANGLICAN
CHAMCOOK, N.B.

T his pretty little church dates back to 1846. The pink colour of the stone is very effectively brought out by the beige-pink trim and red roof.

Roman Catholic Mission Chapel
Brigus South, Nfld.

This tiny church with its defiant bright red trim is huddled against a rocky hill in Brigus South, which has — like so many of Newfoundland's outports — a perfect natural harbour.

The building is unusual in that it combines the Roman arch over the entrance with Gothic windows. The windows have narrow eyebrow-like decorations over them, a feature I noticed frequently along the east coast of Newfoundland and on Prince Edward Island as well. I was particularly struck by the little cemetery, which suggested to me the fragile nature of human life, through the delicate wooden crosses, the skeleton ribs of the boat, and the scaffolding of the pier.

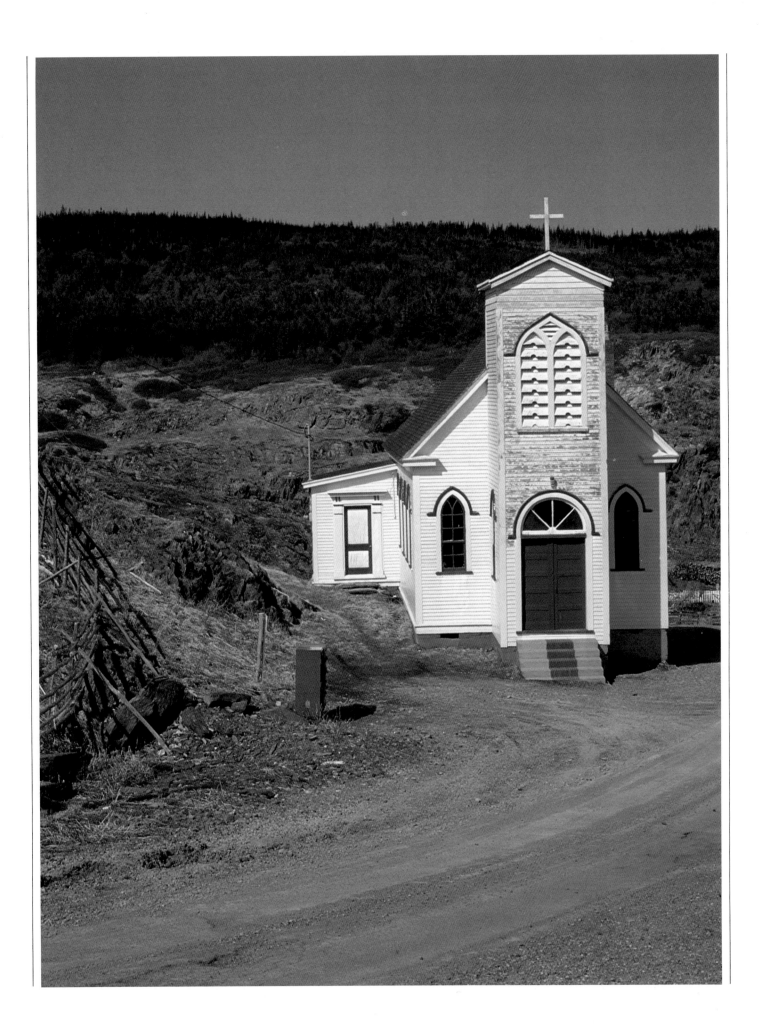

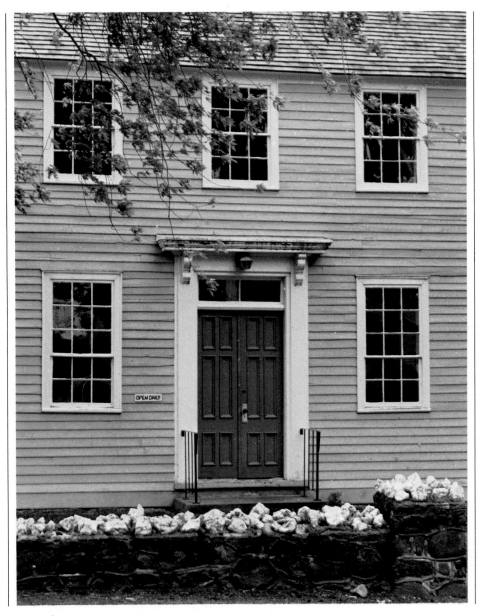

HORTON MEETING HOUSE
HORTON, N.S.

This typical New England–style meeting house was built at the beginning of the nineteenth century by Congregationalist immigrants from the United States. They linked up with the Presbyterians — clergymen were scarce in their new settlement, and the only one available was Presbyterian. The meeting house became known as "The Old Covenanter's Church". As so often happened to these simple rectangular buildings with their symmetrically placed windows, a bell tower was added at a later date — around 1820. The day I passed through Horton the meeting house was locked, and the person who had the key was not at home. This was less frustrating than usual because I was able to stand on some blocks and peer in through a window. The white-painted interior with its box pews and balcony reminded me of St. Andrew's at Niagara-on-the-Lake (see p. 135), but in place of the central pulpit and choir dock there was a simple stand for the pastor's Bible or sermon notes.

This little church on the east shore
of the Nipigon River was originally
known as the Lake Helen Mission
Church. Now Highway 11 North goes
past its door. The photograph was
taken in pouring rain.

Facing ST. MARY'S ROMAN CATHOLIC
GLENDALE, CAPE BRETON ISLAND, N.S.

Unfortunately, when I arrived at St.
Mary's it was drizzling and also
getting dark. The exterior of the
church with its oddly framed Gothic
rosette window is attractive, but I
found the interior even more striking:
it has a U-shaped balcony with a handsome railing, and the white altar is set
off by a blue background and covered
with a red altar cloth with a design of
white doves in a fleur-de-lis border.

Facing UKRAINIAN RUSSIAN ORTHODOX
NEAR LEDUC, ALTA.

This old beauty stands at a junction known as Rabbit Hill. It's painted cream and tangerine, with saints painted in the alcoves. Unusual features of this church are the columns, which stand out in relief on the sides and at the corners of the twin towers, and the almost classical wooden trim under the eaves.

Above PRIMITIVE METHODIST
TORONTO, ONT.

The Primitive Methodists opposed what they termed "clerical tyranny" and supported equal representation for laymen. In 1884 they were absorbed into the Methodist Church. This little church, built in 1873, is now sandwiched between skyscrapers on Finch Avenue, just east of the 404 expressway. Fortunately it is safe from the bulldozer, as it has been declared a historical site. When funds are available it will be restored and in time it may again be used for special occasions and services during the warmer months. It will in any case remain a symbol of our past in the midst of rapid growth and change.

Facing HATLEY UNITED
HATLEY, P.Q.

T his church, built in 1836, was originally Methodist. It resembles the
New England meeting house with its
simple lines, multi-paned and symmetrically placed colonial windows, and
narrow horizontal siding. I was amused
by the fake columns at the corners of
the building; they are almost flush
with the walls and make no pretence of
supporting anything.

Above OUR LADY OF VICTORY,
ROMAN CATHOLIC
INUVIK, N.W.T.

T he inspiration for this much-
photographed church is obviously
the igloo. It was built in 1954, on a
gravel base on top of the muskeg, and
has remained surprisingly stable. I was
disappointed to find that the church
was locked and the priest away as I had
heard that it contained some remark-
able paintings by an Inuit girl of the
stations of the cross.

SOUTH STANSTEAD UNITED
(ORIGINALLY CHURCH OF SCOTLAND)
ROCK ISLAND, P.Q.

Whoever built this board-and-batten church must have loved triangles, not only do the patterns incorporate triangles, but the battens themselves are triangular in section. This picture shows the triangle, symbol of the Trinity, set within the circle, symbol of unity and infinity. Inside the church I was startled to find the altar flanked by both the Canadian maple-leaf flag and the "Stars and Stripes". The town of Rock Island straddles the border — some houses are actually half in Canada and half in the United States — and the missionary funds, like the congregation, are shared between the two countries.

ST. JOSEPH'S MISSION CHAPEL
YALE, B.C.

I went to Yale to photograph one of the oldest Anglican churches in British Columbia, but found it so overgrown by large trees and shrubs in full leaf that it was impossible to get the type of shot I wanted. I settled instead for St. Joseph's, which is set right down in the Fraser Canyon on the outskirts of the town. This chapel appealed to me because it made me think of Emily Carr's painting "Indian Church", although St. Joseph's is towered over by mountains rather than by trees.

Yale is now a quiet village but it was once, I was told, "the busiest city west of Chicago and north of San Francisco". In 1858 some California miners discovered gold on Hill's Bar, a mile and a half south of Yale on the Fraser River, and almost overnight the small community known as Fort Yale blossomed into a city of over 20,000. There was dancing in the streets as well as in the ballrooms of various hotels, and in the liveliest place, "Panama Lil's", miners gambled with fifty-dollar gold slugs under flickering oil lamps set in crystal chandeliers and celebrated their successes with champagne or bemoaned their losses with beer.

70

There's a lot to look at in this white church with its grey trim and black roof: the steeple roof (which reminds me of a Puritan's hat), the knobs, the unusual brackets, the scalloped board, the eye-like patterns within the top half of the Gothic windows, the horizontal wainscotting, and the wrought-iron railing with its missing sections; to all this the half-opened maple leaves add their own patterns.

On the way to Batoche I happened upon this striking church in a field alongside the highway. The simplicity of the side wall running parallel to the highway appealed to me immediately, and I also liked the slight touch of decoration in the peaks of the gables.

Another thing I noticed here and saw again elsewhere in Saskatchewan and Alberta was the simple net or lace curtains used to filter the sunlight. Unfortunately this church, like most that stand alone in the country, was locked.

Above CHIEF'S SPIRIT HOUSE
HAZELTON, B.C.

Facing ST. BARNABAS, BISHOP BOMPAS
MEMORIAL, ANGLICAN
MOOSEHIDE, YUKON

I saw a number of burial-ground spirit houses — on a hill overlooking Whitehorse, above the road to Haines Junction in the Yukon, high on a hill in northern British Columbia. These are the homes the Indians build for the shades of their loved ones to dwell in. Some have fences around them, others have curtains in the windows. (Someone told me that the spirits of the dead join other souls in heaven or the happy hunting grounds, but that a kind of shadow remains behind to be cared for by the family.) Passers-by are asked not to take pictures of burial grounds, but this one spirit house has been moved to the Indian village at Hazelton so that visitors can look at it and photograph it if they wish. It stands alone on low ground near the place where the Skeena and Bulkley rivers meet.

Bishop Bompas and his wife were first posted to Fort Simpson in what is now the Northwest Territories, in 1874, but the bishop was responsible for a huge territory. It's hard to conceive how he and the other early clergymen of the north covered the vast distances they did by dog-sled, snow-shoes, and canoe; today, travelling by car, helicopter, boat, and plane, I found the miles unbelievably long and lonely at times. Bishop Bompas died at Carcross in the Yukon, his last posting, in 1906, and in 1908 the Indians at the mission in Moosehide showed their appreciation and respect by building this church in his memory. A sign beside the church tells of the various Indian friends who helped the visiting clergymen; one is described as "made Deacon lost second eye hunting caribou — yet still performs inspiring ministry." The sign goes on to say that the government withdrew funding for the local school in 1957; although no date is given, St. Barnabas was probably abandoned by 1960.

SEVENTH DAY ADVENTIST
ST. JOHN'S, NFLD.

This church, originally Congregational, sits on the side of a hill in St. John's. It's really a little large to be included here, but I couldn't bring myself to pass up this wonderful door.

ST. PETER'S–ST. JOHN'S, ANGLICAN
BADDECK, CAPE BRETON ISLAND, N.S.

The rather unusual steeple on this little church is known locally as "Gibbon's Steeple", and it has been copied elsewhere in the province. The designer of the steeple was the first Anglican minister to the area of Baddeck and Neils Harbour, the Reverend Simon Gibbon. He urged the people of a village known as "little Baddeck" to build a church of their own (an Anglican chapel, St. John's, had been built in Big Baddeck in 1853). Under his direction, St. Peter's was completed in 1883. Gibbon then provided the baptismal font; he went on a lecture tour in Great Britain and brought back with him a hollowed-out Saxon stone with an open-mouthed head carved in relief on its side, and had it mounted on a stand for baptisms. The stained-glass windows behind the altar were donated by Mrs. Alexander Graham Bell, from a private chapel in a home she had owned in Washington, D. C. When St. John's was dismantled in 1965 the congregation joined that of St. Peter's, which has since been known as St. Peter's–St. John's.

UKRAINIAN GREEK ORTHODOX
SIRKO, MAN.

Sirko, a small hamlet south of Sundown in south-western Manitoba, is probably best known for this old wooden church built in 1909-10. It has a delightfully simple, almost primitive quality to it, especially noticeable in close-ups of the window and door.

Above St. Anne's Roman Catholic
Falher, Alta.

This derelict building standing in the middle of a field looks more like a
deserted house than a church, and in fact its life as a church was brief. Pioneers
came to the area in 1912-13 and built the original St. Anne's, a tiny log chapel which
burned down a couple of years later. It was replaced in 1915 by this building, but a
short four years later the railway went through, two and a half miles north-west of
the village. The villagers moved to be near the railroad and once again they built
themselves a new church, while St. Anne's was converted into a house and lived in
for many years before it was finally abandoned. But the story is not over yet: when
I was in Falher, the mayor assured me that funds had already been raised to restore
"St. Anne's in the Field", as it is the oldest church in the district.

Facing Layer-Cake Church, Anglican and
Presbyterian
Bath, Ont.

This board-and-batten building, which dates back to about 1850, is referred to
locally as the "layer-cake church" because for several years the Anglicans used
the upper storey for their services, while their own church underwent extensive
repairs, and the Presbyterians used the ground floor for theirs. The tastes of these
two denominations are, I think, reflected in the different windows of the gable.

PRIVATE CHAPEL
THE ACADEMY, ROCKWOOD, ONT.

Sculptor Josef Drenters, who undertook the herculean task of restoring the forty-two-room Rockwood Academy (a historical building and museum in which he now lives), also built this fine little private chapel and the stone wall which connects it to the main building. The chapel has a lamb on its weathervane as a symbol of peace and caring. The door opens into a simple stone interior with a single metal cross on the end wall, designed and made by the sculptor's father.

82

ST. ANTOINE DE PADOUE, ROMAN CATHOLIC
BATOCHE, SASK.

The rectory at Batoche was built in 1883 and the church the following year. It was here that Métis leader Louis Riel fought his last battle in 1885; he surrendered in this very rectory and was tried for treason and hanged that same year. A nearby museum contains many old photographs and artefacts that present the history, life, and struggle of the Métis in the west.

This little church on Conception Bay is unusual because it has its back to the sea. Nearly all the small churches on Newfoundland's coast look out across the water, but this one faces the road and is named accordingly. When I was in Topsail this church was being threatened with demolition, as a new church had been built, but a group had already formed to save it and I imagine it has survived.

ST. GEORGE'S ANGLICAN
PETTY HARBOUR, NFLD.

When I was on the plane to Newfoundland I asked a New-
foundlander sitting next to me how
the Newfoundland dog originated. He
explained that Petty Harbour water
dogs, which look like black Labrador
retrievers, had mated with huge Great
Pyrenees brought over by the Port-
uguese, resulting in the large, handsome dogs now known as Newfound-
lands. On the day I went to Petty Harbour it was blowing and raining and
utterly miserable — even the church
looked forlorn in this cold, bleak
landscape — and I didn't see a living
soul. Not even a dog ventured out.

ST. GEORGE'S ANGLICAN
BRIGUS, NFLD.

This church has what would be described in Ontario as a mother-in-law door: if you step through it, you step into space. The door was obviously intended to be the main entrance of the church, but it requires elaborate steps and railings to be useful, and the parishioners likely found it more practical to run the steps up alongside the building and enter the vestibule from the side. The free-standing bell tower with its Gothic openings is another interesting and unusual feature.

ISLE OF PATMOS PRIVATE CHURCH
BLAINE LAKE, SASK.

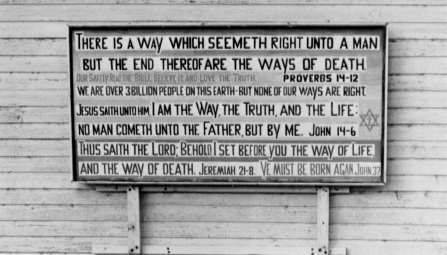

Isaac Theilson, an artist who lives in Borden, Saskatchewan, purchased this building in Blaine Lake from the Anglican Church. He has painted his personal creed — made up primarily of passages from the Bible — on the outside walls. Apparently the name "Isle of Patmos" refers to the time the artist spent in the Greek Islands. Residents of Blaine Lake do not appear to be particularly interested in this eccentric form of evangelism: I made several futile enquiries and in the end I only found the church by driving up and down the village streets. (It's located at the corner of First and Second avenues.) People living nearby told me that all Mr. Theilson wants is for passers-by to read his messages, and in fact one of the first quotations I noticed, above the centre window, was "Blessed be he that readeth".

"BRIGADE HALL"
PEACHLAND, B.C.

This curious building was con-
structed in 1902 as the First Baptist
Church. Its octagonal design is rare in
Canada; I was told that only four such
buildings remain in British Columbia.
In 1958, when the new highway went
through Peachland, it took away most
of the land around the church. A new
Baptist church was built and the old
one became the fire hall, known in
town as the "Brigade Hall". In travelling
around this country I saw many small
churches that had been converted into
homes, meeting halls, township offices,
antique and craft shops, and restau-
rants, but this is the only one I encountered that was turned into a fire hall.

GLENBORO UNITED CHURCH
(FORMERLY WESTMINSTER PRESBYTERIAN)
GLENBORO, MAN.

Glenboro's original Presbyterian church was built around 1889, burned to the ground in 1895, and was replaced within the year by the present building. In 1925 many Presbyterian congregations merged with the Methodists and Congregationalists to form the United Church of Canada.

St. Vincent de Paul Roman Catholic
Niagara-on-the-Lake, Ont.

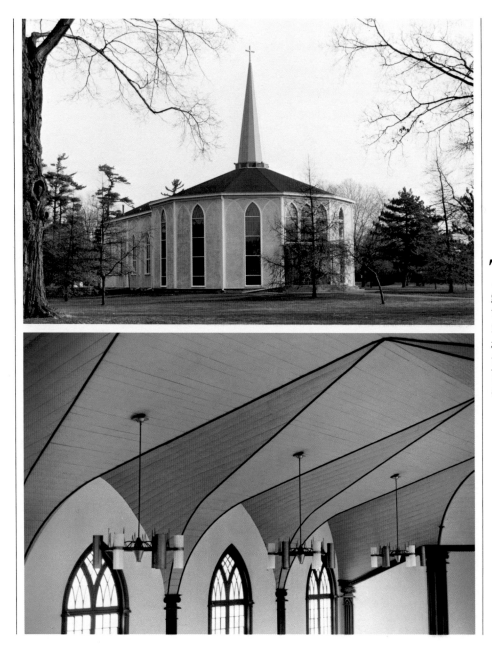

The original St. Vincent's, built in 1834, can be seen across the graveyard. I found it quite exciting with its attractive wooden ceiling and its bright blue interior. The polygonal addition dates from the sixties; from the outside it looks a little incongruous but inside the new and the old blend quite effectively.

St. George's Anglican
Jacksons Point, Ont.

IN LOVING MEMORY OF
STEPHEN BUTLER LEACOCK
BORN DEC. 30, 1869
DIED MAR. 28, 1944
ROSAMOND MARY BUTLER
LEACOCK
WIFE OF HARRY D. EDWARDS
BORN MAY 28, 1884
DIED MAY 28, 1849
CHARLES JOHN GLADSTONE
LEACOCK
BORN DEC. 6, 1871
DIED AUG. 26, 1951

MAZO
DE LA ROCHE
1888 — 1961

DEATH INTERRUPTS ALL THAT IS MORTAL

St. George's, referred to locally as the "Sibbald Memorial Church", was built in memory of Susan Sibbald, in 1877, by her seven sons. It is made of stone and resembles an English manor church. Its ties with Britain are underlined by a description I was given of Captain Thomas Sibbald, a retired naval officer and the son most interested in supervising the construction. It is said that he would appear on the site every day and "do the rounds" just as he had done when he was serving on a British man-of-war. If all was satisfactory he would give the foreman the order to "Carry on," and the foreman would reply "Aye aye, Sir"; then, at eight bells, Captain Sibbald would give each of the workmen a ration of rum and they would proceed to drink the Queen's health.

Today this little church on the south shore of Lake Simcoe is interesting not only for its own story, but because Stephen Leacock and Mazo de la Roche are buried in the churchyard. These two, perhaps the best-known Canadian writers during the first part of this century, both loved Lake Simcoe and spent many summers at family cottages in the area. The Leacock tombstone is near the church in front of a large pine planted by Captain Sibbald, and the de la Roche grave is by the lake.

CHRIST CHURCH ANGLICAN
FREDERICTON, N.B.

The distinguishing feature of this church is obviously the bell-tower façade, but what appealed to me even more was the simplicity of the stained-glass window below, which was donated by the Women's Auxiliary. The doors of the main entrance are unusual — they are completely covered by an ornate iron pattern which appears to be purely decorative but actually incorporates the hinges.

Built in 1861 on the shores of the Red River near Selkirk, St. Clement's is a nicely proportioned stone church. Its handsome square tower is topped, surprisingly, by a weathercock; such ornaments are usually reserved for the spires of steeples.

This unusual octagonal church was built originally as the second Congregational church of Eramosa County. Like many buildings in the Guelph area it is made of stone. The interior is unusual in that pews are arranged almost all the way around the pulpit, so that it's possible for worshippers to face other members of the congregation.

Above WAYSIDE CHAPEL
ON THE NORTH SIDE OF
CROW'S NEST PASS, ALTA.

Facing ST. STEPHEN'S ANGLICAN
NEAR VICTORIA, B.C.

This little chapel, which urges the passing motorist to drive carefully and to take time to enter and say a prayer, is typical of a number I came across in my travels. It seats about six and is non-denominational. In the days when people travelled the trails on horseback or snow-shoes, wayside chapels offered the tired and often frozen traveller a refuge and a resting-place. There's a famous one outside Drumheller, Alberta, which boasts that it can seat ten thousand people — six at a time — and another can be found on the west side of the beautiful drive along the gorge between Niagara Falls and Niagara-on-the-Lake, but for me the most interesting one is in British Columbia (see p. 153).

Built in 1812, St. Stephen's is the oldest Anglican church in British Columbia that still stands on its original site and has continued its services, Sunday after Sunday, all through the years. The spruce saplings that were planted on either side of the entrance now dwarf the church. Many of the old trees in the churchyard are covered in Spanish moss, and its long grey wisps created an eerie atmosphere, even though it was a beautiful fall day with sunlight streaming through the yellow maple leaves. St. Stephen's is a little difficult to find: it's about a quarter of a mile off the West Saanich Road, between Brentwood and the airport.

St. Andrew's United
(Originally Presbyterian)
Williamstown, Ont.

Built under the direction of the Reverend John Bethune, a Presbyterian clergyman who had served as a Loyalist chaplain during the American Revolution, the stone church of St. Andrew's replaced a log one built in 1786. The new St. Andrew's was begun in 1812 and took six years to complete. It is built of uncoursed rubble stonework; the original French stonemason, François-Xavier Rochileaux, died before his task was done and the job was taken over by an English stonemason, John Kirby, who added British touches like the Palladian arches over the windows. The trim around the windows and along the eaves is a soft olive-green which complements the stonework, and there is an elaborate iron fence surrounding the churchyard. Williamstown lies north-east of Cornwall.

ST. BERNARD ROMAN CATHOLIC
STE. MARGUERITE STATION, P.Q.

The type of stonework in this church might well be called "flagstone style" as the stones have a flat surface and are arranged in a random manner. The mortar used to join them has been whitened in order to make the pattern of the arrangement stand out. St. Bernard's has three dormer windows on either side of the roof, and these dormers, plus the lowness of the building and the way it is landscaped and fitted into the hill, give the church a chalet appearance well suited to its Laurentian setting.

ST. STEPHEN'S ANGLICAN
CHAMBLY, P.Q.

Chambly, once a garrison town, lies about fifteen miles east of Montreal, on the west bank of the Richelieu River. St. Stephen's was built in 1820, to serve the garrison, rather than the townspeople who were mainly of Scottish Presbyterian stock. The exterior is an interesting forerunner of biculturalism: the front with its gracious porch, doorway, and multi-paned Georgian windows on either side is distinctively British, while the back has the arched windows and rounded chancel common in the early Roman Catholic churches of Quebec. (It is in fact strikingly similar to the Roman Catholic St.-François-de-Sales, built around 1734, which still stands on Ile d'Orléans.) The designers of St. Stephen's were British, but clearly they were not impervious to the French architecture surrounding them.

ST. MICHAEL'S ROMAN CATHOLIC
FORT RAE, N.W.T.

The original church at Fort Rae, near Yellowknife, was built in 1907 and was replaced in 1925 by the church shown here. Like so many Roman Catholic churches and missions in the north, it belongs to the Oblate order. The interior is flooded with light from the high Roman-arched windows along the sides and in the steeple. It is also very colourful, as children's paintings are hung around the walls and a children's mural decorates the altar.

109

WAYSIDE CHAPEL
ILE D'ORLÉANS, P.Q.

This tiny chapel beside the road along the north shore is made of rubble-stone stuccoed over and then whitewashed. This is the only time that I saw the rounded-end design used in miniature. Like so many other wayside and processional chapels that I noticed as I travelled in Quebec, it is no longer in use; it is boarded up and badly in need of restoration.

WAYSIDE CHAPEL, ROMAN CATHOLIC
LES EBOULEMENTS, P.Q.

This chapel stands beside the Rivière du Moulin on the north shore highway, not far from Ile aux Coudres. It is completely boarded up, and the tall weeds around it suggest it has been neglected for a long time.

SACRE COEUR, ROMAN CATHOLIC
TORS COVE, NFLD.

This church on Newfoundland's east coast was built in 1900, at the end of the Victorian era, and its vast fake buttresses remind me irresistibly of the imposing bustles of that age.

Right PROCESSIONAL CHAPEL,
ROMAN CATHOLIC
NEUVILLE, P.Q.

This little stone chapel with its shut-
tered windows and louvered fan
over the door is located on the north
shore of the St. Lawrence about twenty
miles up the river from Quebec City. It
was built around 1730 for use in cere-
monial processions. I am intrigued by
the "door-and-a-half" within the
Roman arch of the entrance; I wonder
if the present door replaced a larger
original one.

Facing ALL SAINTS ANGLICAN
NEAR GONDOLA POINT, N.B.

This little wooden church with its
cream and brown trim sits beside
the sea on the Kingston Peninsula
just south of Gondola Point. It was
built in 1885.

Facing LYCH-GATE, NECROPOLIS CHAPEL AND CEMETERY
TORONTO, ONT.

Above LYCH-GATE, ST. ANDREW'S
GRIMSBY, ONT.

Below LYCH-GATE, ST. MARY'S
FULFORD HARBOUR, SALTSPRING ISLAND, B.C.

I have been told many stories about lych-gates: that in past centuries a Roman Catholic and an Anglican could not be married in an English church but could, in some parishes, hold the wedding in the lych-gate; that coffins were halted and opened at this point to ensure that no forbidden body — a suicide, for example — was smuggled into consecrated ground; even that coffins were opened within the gate to let any evil spirits escape before the entry into the church for funeral services. "Lych" is derived from an Old English word meaning "corpse", and lych-gates are also called coffin-gates, so it's curious that in the twentieth century they have acquired a romantic image — some have sheltered benches that make them tempting "lovers' gates", and bridal parties often choose them as picturesque backgrounds for wedding photographs.

HOLY ROSARY MISSION CHAPEL,
ROMAN CATHOLIC
PORTUGAL COVE, NFLD.

This extraordinary church was built in 1915. Its onion dome, twin towers, and spoke-filled circles on top of the windows reminded me of the Russian and Greek Orthodox churches on the Prairies, while the cross above the entrance recalled the Indian mission churches in British Columbia.

Facing CLARENCE UNITED BAPTIST
CLARENCE, N.S.

This church in the Annapolis Valley attracted my attention with its handsome bell tower.

Above ROMAN CATHOLIC CHURCH
PEACHLAND, B.C.

Many families of fruit-pickers and growers have moved from the south-western United States into the Okanagan Valley. This church reflects their Spanish and Mexican origins.

Above MARTIN'S MEETING HOUSE,
MENNONITE
JUST NORTH OF WATERLOO, ONT.

This meeting house received its name from the Martin family, who donated the land on which it was built in 1831. When this photograph was taken, a group of Mennonites known as Markhamites were attending a meeting. (They are called Markhamites because their ancestors originally settled in Markham, Ontario, before moving westward to the Kitchener-Waterloo area.) Hundreds of black cars, most with their chrome painted a humble black, were parked in the large parking lot and hitching area along the side and back of the cemetery. Martin's Meeting House is also used by Old Order Mennonites, but I was told that their meetings do not follow any regular schedule — if they did, crowds would gather to watch and photograph the procession of horse-drawn buggies or sleighs. Our energy problems need not worry Old Order Mennonites, for they live today as their ancestors lived a hundred years ago, without electricity, cars, or other modern conveniences. One Sunday I happened to pass Martin's Meeting House as the Old Order were leaving. The women, in their black cloaks, bonnets, and stockings, formed a solid island of black as they stood in front waiting for their men to bring the buggies around. I turned the corner and watched from the side road as the men removed horse-blankets, untied horses, and backed their buggies out. The older men drove sedately, but the bachelors had spirited horses which often reared up, fighting the bit, and took off stepping high and fast like pacers on the Fort Erie track; they reminded me of other young men in their Mustangs or Corvettes.

Facing PROTESTANT CHURCH
STE. ADÈLE, P.Q.

This little stucco church is supported mainly by local residents, but it is also attended by many skiers and summer visitors as it is just outside the entrance to the Chanteclerc resort.

Facing St. John's United
Strathlorne, Cape Breton Island, N.S.

This trim little church with its red roof, grey steps, and attractive steeple topped with an unusual weathervane is just off the Cabot Trail, on your right as you head north to Inverness.

Near left Derelict Chapel,
Roman Catholic
near Lillooet, B.C.

This tiny, silvered "leaning tower of Pisa" can be found, if it hasn't already tumbled down, on the Reservation alongside Seton Lake Road near Lillooet. It is set against a tall blue mountain and, like many small churches in Canada, it will be lost beyond recovery unless restorations are begun very soon.

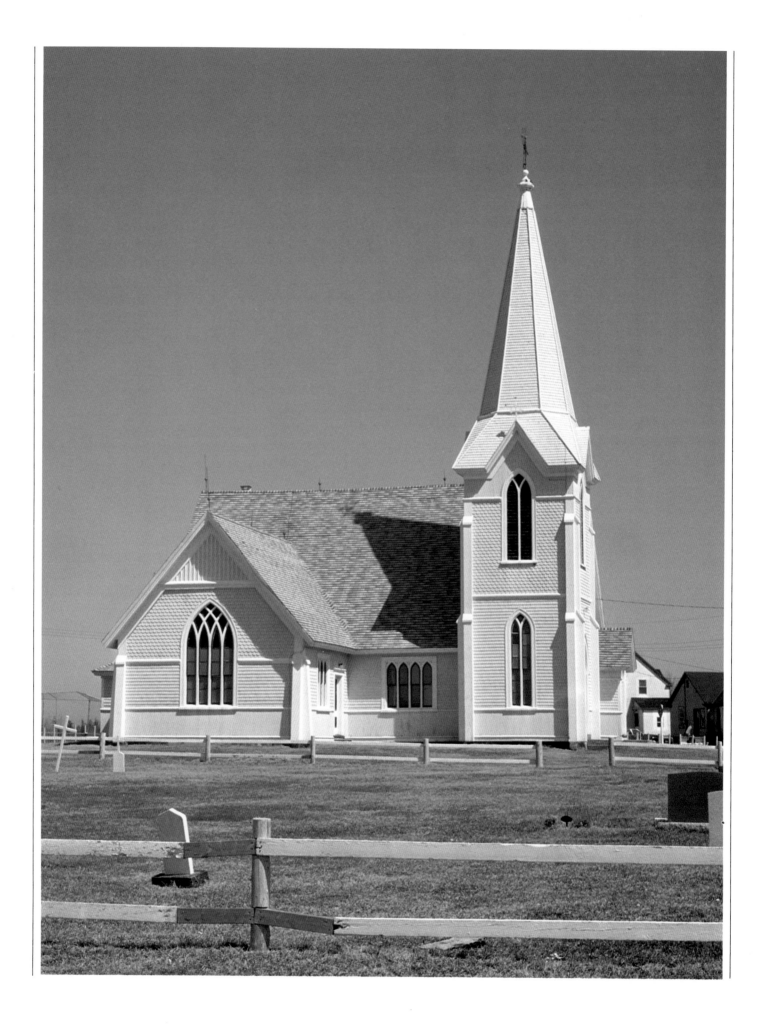

St. Anne's Roman Catholic
Lennox Island, P.E.I.

St. Anne's is beautifully set on a point of land on the Micmac Indian Reserve. While on the Reserve I met an elderly woman who told me that her grand-father Joe Bernard, and his friend Joe Knockwood, had helped to build the present church to replace an earlier one on the same site. The old woman spoke Micmac but her daughter, who was with her, admitted that while she herself understood the language, she could not speak it.

HOLY FAMILY ROMAN CATHOLIC
FERNIE, B.C.

T his red brick church built in 1911
stands at the half-way point of
Crow's Nest Pass, the most southerly
pass through the Canadian Rockies. I
couldn't help wondering what had
happened to the tower's bell.

SANDY COVE, N.S.

I n this bird's-eye view of the seaside
village, one of the town's three
churches dominates the scene.

SALVATION ARMY CHAPEL
CANYON CITY, B.C.

The first time I crossed this swaying footbridge held up by fishnets, I was petrified. I had been told that, on a gusty January night only a month before, the bridge had turned right over in a high wind. Fortunately no one was on it at the time or they would have been hurled down into the fast-moving waters of the Nass. The mercury was down to about 35°F, and as I crossed clutching my camera pack the planks creaked and cracked as if they were about to snap. Below, sheets of ice worn thin as bridal veils by the swift water swirled their way downstream. When at last I reached the other side I was not surprised to find a Salvation Army chapel there — the Sally Ann has a reputation for turning up in difficult times and difficult places.

Architect James Cooper designed St. Andrews, built in 1831, to replace the original Church of Scotland which had been burned by the Americans in the War of 1812. In 1938 the church was restored by prominent architect Eric Arthur, who carefully followed Cooper's original plans. The red brick is quite handsome, with its white portico, Doric columns, and tall arched windows, but what really appealed to me was the inside, which is brilliant with light even on hazy days. Looking down from the balcony, I could imagine large families being led to their box stalls, and ushers latching the pew gates behind them. The interior is mainly a composition in white and black, with red introduced through the pew cushions and flags. When I attended a service I discovered that the organist and choir serve as the final touch to this striking scene, for their gowns are cerulean blue with gold hoods.

BETH ISRAEL SYNAGOGUE
EDENBRIDGE, SASK.

Edenbridge, a small community on the Carrot River north of Brookby, was founded in 1906 by Russian Jews who had come to Canada via South Africa to take up the Canadian government's offer of inexpensive farmland. Beth Israel Synagogue was built in 1908 and by the 1920s it was supported by fifty families. When the settlement gained a post office, a town name was required. The government rejected as "unsuitable" any name suggesting Jews or Israel but accepted the pleasant-sounding "Edenbridge". The joke was on them: the name is a pun on *Yidden* bridge, or "Jews' Bridge". The synagogue is no longer in use, as the families who supported it have moved to the cities, but it is cared for as a historical site.

ST. GEORGE'S ANGLICAN
HEAD OF ST. MARGARETS BAY, N.S.

This church is perched precariously right on the margin of the bay. After I had seen so many white churches, St. George's with its dark chocolate-coloured shingles and cream trim was a welcome change.

This derelict church, like a number of others, stands all by itself out on the Prairies, the only remaining sign of a vanished ghost town.

DUNVEGAN MISSION, ROMAN CATHOLIC
ON THE PEACE RIVER NEAR FAIRVIEW, ALTA.

This reconstructed log church stands near the spot where the original log church stood in the nineteenth century, at what was then known as Fort Dunvegan. The *coureurs du bois* began to travel this area in the 1770s, and the Roman Catholic missionaries were not far behind.

ST. ANTHONY'S ROMAN CATHOLIC (*left*)
& ST. MARY'S ANGLICAN (*facing*)
NORTH BATTLEFORD, SASK.

These two tiny chapels were removed from their original sites in the now-vanished hamlets of Redfield and Lilac, and were rebuilt as much as necessary in the Pioneer Village and museum on the outskirts of North Battleford. The board-walks, which were common in the past, are rarely found these days except in reconstructed villages and forts. I found myself wishing that they were more popular today as I squelched my way through a particularly damp and muddy prairie spring — my boots were always thick with gumbo, and my car came to resemble a hippopotamus wallow.

MURRAY UNITED
NICOLA, B.C.

This stark building, the first Presbyterian church in British Columbia, was built in 1876. It was named after its first minister, the Reverend George Murray, who had come to Nicola from his native Scotland. In the churchyard is a fenced-in double grave that made me think of a double bed.

MENNONITE MEETING HOUSE
STEINBACH, MAN.

Mennonites began migrating to Manitoba in 1874, as a result of persecution by Czar Alexander II of Russia, and by 1877 some seven thousand Mennonites had settled there. Today Mennonite communities and churches can be found all across the west and, as I mentioned in the foreword, there is even a Chinese Mennonite church in Vancouver. The meeting house in Steinbach, Manitoba, is one of the handsomest I encountered. It was built in 1881. The plain shutters are its only embellishment, and they are probably functional, used to protect the windows during severe storms. Inside, the bench-like pews enforce good posture and the unadorned pulpit placed squarely at the end of the centre aisle commands attention. Men sit on one side of the aisle, I was told, and women on the other. Offering boxes are placed inconspicuously at the entrance as it is felt that passing open offering plates might encourage "making a show".

HUTTERITE MEETING HOUSE
NEAR RAYMOND, ALTA.

Only the Hutterite meeting houses in southern Alberta struck me as simpler and more austere. The Hutterites, like the Mennonites, are descended from the sixteenth-century Anabaptist movement. They are one of the most recent minority groups to immigrate to Canada, as they came in via the north-western United States where they had first settled. They live in communes, farming vast tracts of land with modern machinery and old-fashioned zeal; they live in impeccable row houses, share a communal dining hall, and have very simple meeting houses. The one I photographed was more colourful and warmer than most: patterned linoleum on the floor and benches contributed a sunny yellow and deep gold to the otherwise bleak room with its aluminum windows, acoustic tiles, and fluorescent lights.

SHIN BUDDHIST TEMPLE
RAYMOND, ALTA.

As early as 1904 Japanese settlers came east across the Rockies and settled in Raymond, many to work in the sugar beet industry. In 1929 the Buddhists purchased this building, which had originally been a school, from the Mormons, and three years later the Buddhists established a co-op store to help raise money for remodelling the building as a temple. When Japan entered the Second World War, and Japanese Canadians were stripped of their properties and forced into camps and communities away from the coast, some of them came to Raymond. They brought with them an intricately carved and very valuable altar, all covered in gold leaf, which had originally been brought from Japan. In my travels across Canada I saw several Buddhist temples, but this one in Raymond had the most interesting history.

"Log Cathedral", Anglican
Whitehorse, Yukon

This church, which is unusually large for the north, now houses a museum and is open only during the milder months. It is connected with most of the outstanding Anglican clergymen of the north, including Bishop Isaac Stringer. Stringer is known as "the bishop who ate his own boots" — winter overtook him as he was travelling from Fort McPherson to Dawson, and he was reduced to boiling his boots for seven hours and then baking them on hot stones to make them edible. He survived the ordeal; just one year later, four Mounties lost their lives on the same route, despite eating their dogs and even their harnesses in an attempt to stay alive. When I was photographing St. Andrew's church in Grimsby, Ontario, I met a minister who had served at the "Log Cathedral" in the fifties. He told me that a nativity scene which he and others sculptured out of snow and ice just before Christmas lasted right through till Easter. When I photographed the "Log Cathedral" in February, Whitehorse was shrouded in ice fog and the temperature stood at 55°F , under a noonday sun that looked like a full moon.

NON-DENOMINATIONAL CHAPEL
USK, B.C.

This wayside chapel on the south side of Highway 16, just east of Terrace in the Skeena Valley, was built as the centennial project of the Christian Reformed Church of Terrace. It is known locally as the "floating Bible chapel", and is a small replica of the pioneer church that stood in Usk prior to the flood of 1936. The original church was built for a popular Anglican priest, Canon T. J. Marsh, in the year of Canada's Confederation. The little church at Usk, like many others in outlying areas and the north, was truly non-denominational: the canon himself was often away, travelling around his wide territory, and congregations were glad to welcome any clergymen who were passing through — whether they were Roman or Anglo Catholic or Protestant mattered little. The legend of the floating Bible grew out of the flood that occurred on May 31, 1936, when the Skeena River burst over its banks and wiped out the entire village of Usk. The church and everything in it was ruined except for the Bible. Evidently this had been left open on a small pine table; the table floated around on the flood waters inside the church, and the Bible riding on top of it escaped without a mark.

WEST DUMFRIES WESLEYAN CHAPEL
PARIS PLAINS, ONT.

Levi Boughton, an American stonemason from New York, introduced
this linear type of pebble or cobble-
stone work to Brant County when he
arrived in 1838. In Paris, Ontario, I
stumbled upon a church, a house, and a
wall all done in Boughton's style. I am
told there are several others in that
area, but it's unlikely that any are more
attractive than this little Methodist
chapel at Paris Plains. The close-up of
the door reveals how the pebbles,
about the size of eggs, are carefully
arranged in rows.

ST. JOHN'S PRESBYTERIAN
BELFAST, P.E.I.

I n 1803 Thomas Douglas, Lord Selkirk, succeeded in bringing three
shiploads of settlers from his native
Scotland to Prince Edward Island. He
had acquired 80,000 acres on the shores
of Northumberland Strait, reclaimed
by the government from absentee
landlords who had failed to bring settlers to the land — a condition of their
grants of 1767. For twenty years Lord
Selkirk's settlers were busy clearing
the evergreen forests and building
homesteads and schools. In 1823, under
the guidance of the Reverend John
MacLennan, they were finally able to
build the church of their dreams: St.
John's Presbyterian at Belfast. Today St.
John's stands, impeccably cared for, in
the midst of a vast churchyard full of
tombstones. The strikingly tiered
"Christopher Wren" steeple, eighty-
five feet high, is a magnificent symbol
of the achievement of the early Selkirk
settlers, while I saw a touch of their
enduring humour on the bulletin
board at the side of the church: "An
old woman had only two teeth, but she
thanked the Lord that they met."

ST. THOMAS ANGLICAN
ST. JOHN'S, NFLD.

St. Thomas, opened on September 21, 1836, is referred to locally as the "old Garrison Church" because it used to serve the troops from the British garrison. The interior of the church intrigued me particularly: it is all in dark wood, and almost in the centre is a beautifully carved pulpit, standing out like one of those steep, tall islands off the coast of Newfoundland. The altar cloth, beautifully embroidered in ivory and gold, showed a lamb standing on a very colourful rainbow. I happened to be in St. John's right after Easter and the "old Garrison", full of Easter lilies, smelled more like a greenhouse than a church.

SHARON TEMPLE, INDEPENDENT QUAKERS
(DAVIDITES)
EAST GWILLIMBURY (SHARON), ONT.

The Sharon Temple or "Temple of the Children of Peace", known locally as "the wedding-cake church", was completed in 1830. The sect who built it were known as Davidites because they had broken away from the Society of Friends (Quakers) to follow David Willson, who had been expelled — according to a young man whose great-grandfather helped Willson build the temple — for speaking out loudly at meetings about the need for music and song and special services in place of the traditional silent worship. The young man told me that Willson's layer-cake plan had originated in some sort of mystical vision he had about music from heaven: he wanted the choir to sing from an upper level, as if from celestial heights. The Davidites did build a conventional meeting house for their regular meetings, but it has not survived. The temple — based on Solomon's temple, or Willson's idea of it — was for festive occasions. On such days as Thanksgiving and May Day, lighted candles were placed in special holders attached to every pane of glass in the twenty-four multi-paned windows of the lower level. Then young women dressed in long white gowns and holding lighted candles sang in the loft and, still singing, made their way down by a steep ladder-like staircase, like a host of angels descending among men. The temple is now used for occasional music festivals.

St. Paul's Anglican (*facing*)
And Rectory (*above*)

Sarah Stringer, wife of Bishop Isaac Stringer, described Dawson as a "veritable Paris". Paris it must have seemed, for she had spent several years on Herschel Island in the Arctic Ocean, where the winters were long and dark and bitterly cold. On Herschel she had known lonely months with her husband away, and there she had given birth to her first child, with her husband as the only attendant. The Anglican rectory reflects the grand lifestyle Dawson experienced during the gold-rush days at the turn of the century. Here the lords and ladies of the north gathered for formal dinners and balls, wearing tails or uniforms tailored in London and New York, or gowns from Paris. Perhaps, the next day, they stopped to pay their calls at the Anglican rectory; one can easily imagine them sitting in elegant groups, conversing and sipping tea, on the spacious veranda and balcony. Certainly prominent visitors to the north were welcomed at the rectory, but so were the native people — after all, the missionaries had shared the difficulties of their lives in the remotest outposts.

This little board-and-batten church with its unusual buttresses was built in 1866. A low stone wall with a lych-gate runs across the front of the property; the gate was built as a memorial for Bishop Lennox Waldren Williams who served the diocese from 1915-1937 and died in 1958. The chapel is used only during the summer months, to serve visitors, and its facilities are shared by Anglican and United clergy.

PENTECOSTAL CHURCH
KILLALOE, ONT.

I was fascinated by the curious decorative fringe on the eaves of this little church, which is now used only during the summer months.

HAY BAY MEETING HOUSE, UNITED
NEAR ADOLPHUSTOWN, ONT.

This meeting house built in 1792 is the oldest Methodist chapel in Upper Canada. It typifies the kind of building put up by the Quakers and Methodists when they moved north into the Maritimes, the Eastern Townships of Quebec, and south-eastern Ontario. It has the plain central entrance and symmetrically placed windows with small panes, and is without any ornamentation; the shutters are functional and their clasps and hinges are simple. Over the years bell towers and elaborate vestibules have been added to many meeting houses, but this one has escaped such additions. A tragic story is revealed inside this simple building: one Sunday morning in August, many years ago, a number of young people piled into a boat to cross the bay and come to morning service. While they lightheart-edly sang their favourite hymns, water seeped unnoticed into the bottom of the overloaded boat. The lower the boat sank in the water, the faster the water poured in through the cracks along the sides. By the time the teenagers finally realized that the situation was serious, it was too late; in spite of the frantic efforts of the youths at the oars, and of a few lads bailing with their hats, the boat sank. Those who could not swim — the majority, in those days — were drowned.

CHURCH OF OUR LADY, ROMAN CATHOLIC
FORT PROVIDENCE, N.W.T.

This church, which is painted white with royal blue trim, was built, I was told, by Gassien Oulette, the same master carpenter who built the church at Fort Rae (see p. 108). He came from Rivière du Loup but never returned to Quebec; he died in the north.

THE GROTTO, ROMAN CATHOLIC
FORT SMITH, N.W.T.

This open-air chapel is evidently a replica of a grotto in France, but with its surrounding circle of spruce it reminded me of an Indian council ring. In my wanderings around the country, I found only two open-air chapels: this example at Fort Smith and a non-denominational one at Half-Moon Bay in the Thousand Islands close to Gananoque, Ontario. The latter is much simpler than this one, for it consists of a large boulder used by visiting clergy as a pulpit or lectern; the congregation remain in their boats tied or anchored in the shelter of the cove.

CHURCH OF ALL SAINTS, ANGLICAN
CANNINGTON MANOR, SASK.

Cannington Manor was founded, as the name suggests, by an English gentleman, Captain Edward Mitchell Pierce, who came to Canada to play the squire after reportedly going bankrupt at home in 1881. Cannington Manor, just north of Carlyle, Saskatchewan, was one of the few settlements where inmigrants were more interested in playing cricket and croquet than in clearing and ploughing the land; according to the story, sixteen homes in Cannington Manor had pianos, and I have visions of oxen hauling all these sensitive instruments over the muddy trails that served as roads in 1880. This little piece of England out on the Prairies lasted for only one generation before the money — and the fun — ran out. All Saints is modelled after an English parish church, with its Gothic windows and the suggestion of quatrefoils in the decorative band around the steeple. The interior is white with dark beams that produce a Tudor effect; unfortunately the graceful coal-oil lamps on the walls have been not so gracefully converted to electricity.

St. Luke's Anglican
Old Crow, Yukon

Old Crow, which is well within the Arctic Circle, is the last post of civilization in the north-western corner of Canada, but both Roman Catholic and Anglican missionaries made their way there across the mountains and muskeg. The pilot gave me only twenty minutes to photograph the churches, while he was unloading and reloading the plane. I did the Roman Catholic one first and then decided to make a run for the Anglican one at the other end of the village. I found the latter unusually interesting because someone had, in a very simple way, added a Gothic touch to the exceptionally low windows. I wondered what the switch was doing by the door: was it for warding off dogs, for reaching up to turn on a light, for use as a disciplinary means in school, or what? But there was no one to ask, and I could hear the pilot revving up his engines in the distance, so I had to leave without finding out the answer.

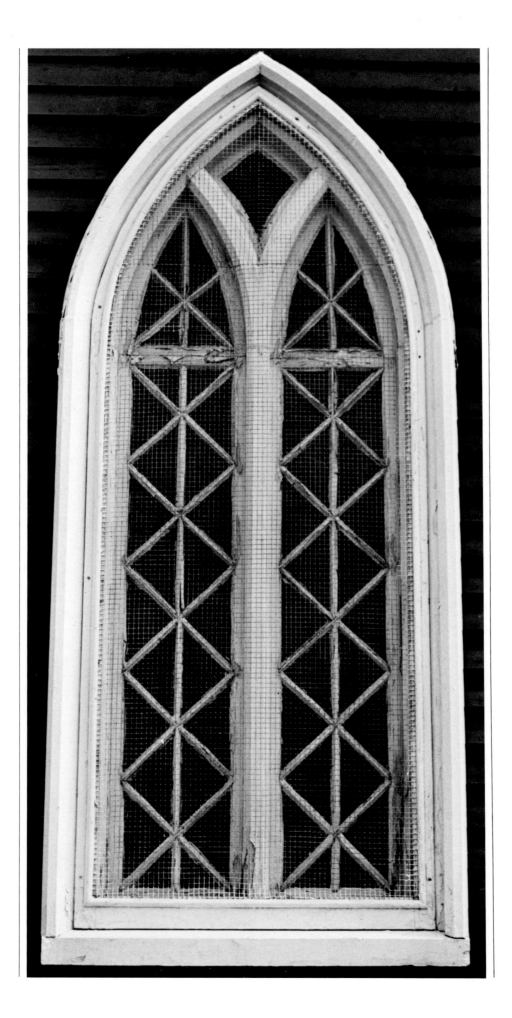

189

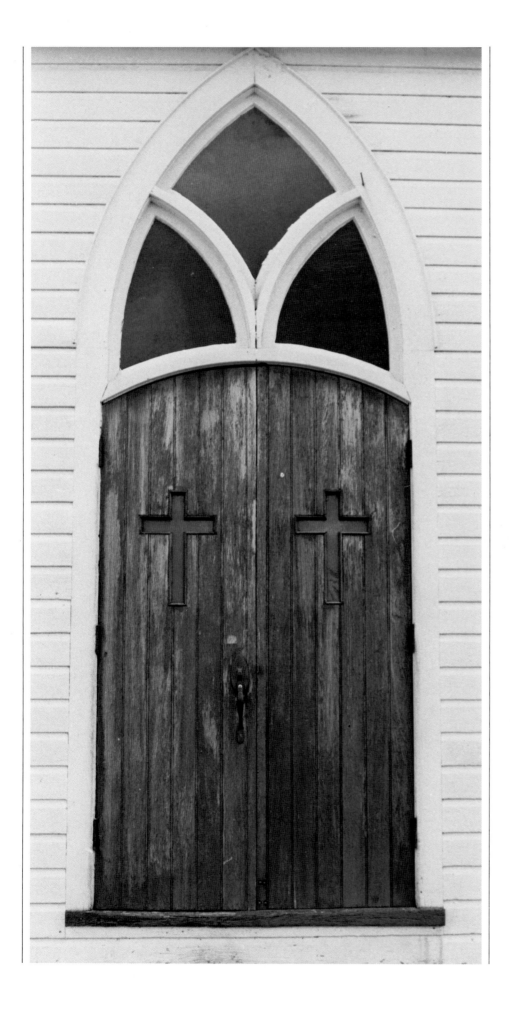